CALVIN COOLIDGE

The Presidents of the United States

George Washington
1789–1797

John Adams
1797–1801

Thomas Jefferson
1801–1809

James Madison
1809–1817

James Monroe
1817–1825

John Quincy Adams
1825–1829

Andrew Jackson
1829–1837

Martin Van Buren
1837–1841

William Henry Harrison
1841

John Tyler
1841–1845

James Polk
1845–1849

Zachary Taylor
1849–1850

Millard Fillmore
1850–1853

Franklin Pierce
1853–1857

James Buchanan
1857–1861

Abraham Lincoln
1861–1865

Andrew Johnson
1865–1869

Ulysses S. Grant
1869–1877

Rutherford B. Hayes
1877–1881

James Garfield
1881

Chester Arthur
1881–1885

Grover Cleveland
1885–1889

Benjamin Harrison
1889–1893

Grover Cleveland
1893–1897

William McKinley
1897–1901

Theodore Roosevelt
1901–1909

William H. Taft
1909–1913

Woodrow Wilson
1913–1921

Warren Harding
1921–1923

Calvin Coolidge
1923–1929

Herbert Hoover
1929–1933

Franklin D. Roosevelt
1933–1945

Harry Truman
1945–1953

Dwight Eisenhower
1953–1961

John F. Kennedy
1961–1963

Lyndon Johnson
1963–1969

Richard Nixon
1969–1974

Gerald Ford
1974–1977

Jimmy Carter
1977–1981

Ronald Reagan
1981–1989

George H. W. Bush
1989–1993

William J. Clinton
1993–2001

George W. Bush
2001–2009

★ ★ ★ ★ ★ ★ ★ ★ ★ ★ ★ ★ ★ ★ ★ ★ ★ ★ ★ ★

CALVIN COOLIDGE

STEVEN OTFINOSKI

 **Marshall Cavendish**
Benchmark
New York

Marshall Cavendish Benchmark
99 White Plains Road
Tarrytown, New York 10591-5502
www.marshallcavendish.us

All Internet addresses were correct at the time of printing.

Library of Congress Cataloging-in-Publication Data

Otfinoski, Steven.
Calvin Coolidge / by Steven Otfinoski
p. cm. — (Presidents and their times)
Summary: "Provides comprehensive information on President Calvin Coolidge and places him
within his historical and cultural context. Also explored are the formative events of his times
and how he responded"—Provided by publisher.
Includes bibliographical references and index.
ISBN 978-0-7614-2836-7
1. Coolidge, Calvin, 1872–1933—Juvenile literature. 2. Presidents—United States—Biography—
Juvenile literature. 3. United States—Politics and government—1923–1929—Juvenile literature.
4. Governors—Massachusetts—Biography—Juvenile literature. I. Title. II. Series.
E792.O86 2009
973.91'5092—dc22
[B]
2007024632

Editor: Christine Florie
Publisher: Michelle Bisson
Art Director: Anahid Hamparian
Series Designer: Alex Ferrari

Photo research by Connie Gardner

Cover photo by The Granger Collection

The photographs in this book are used by permission and through the courtesy of: *Getty Images:*
Hulton Archive, 6, 21, 56, 85 (L); *Digital Railroad:* Andre Jenny, 15; *The Granger Collection:* 13, 22,
35, 41, 43, 46, 53, 60; *Brown Brothers:* 10, 84 (L); *Courtesy of the Forbes Library, Northampton,
Massachusetts:* 8, 9, 17, 84 (R); *Alamy:* The Print Collector, 24; *Corbis:* Bettmann, 11, 26, 27, 30,
32, 34, 38, 44, 48, 54, 58, 61, 68, 70, 74, 75, 76, 79, 85 (R); CORBIS, 3, 18, 64, 65, 67, 83;
Fredrick Schutz, 37; Hulton Deutsch Collections, 52, 59; Conde Nast Archive, 63;
John Carnemolla, 76; *Art Resource:* Snark, 49.

Printed in Malaysia
1 3 5 6 4 2

CONTENTS

A president mostly known for his character rather than his political accomplishments, Calvin Coolidge continues to be a strong representative of his times.

An "Odd Stick"

One

It was after 2 A.M. on a very hot August night in 1923 when Calvin Coolidge, the vice president of the United States, was awakened in bed by his father, John. Coolidge and his wife, Grace, were in the second week of a visit to his father's home in Plymouth Notch, Vermont.

Coolidge was stunned when he learned the reason for this rude awakening. President Warren G. Harding had died suddenly hours earlier at the other end of the country, in San Francisco, California. In this era before instant communications, the dire news had taken all night to reach tiny Plymouth Notch. At 10:30 P.M. a telegram had been wired to Coolidge at White River Junction, about 20 miles away. John Coolidge did not have a telephone, so a telephone exchange worker in Bridgewater drove to Plymouth Notch to deliver the news. His Model T Ford got a flat tire along the way, delaying his arrival.

When the messenger finally arrived, the tiny village was swarming with curious people. Among them was the Vermont congressman Porter Dale, who insisted that the vice president take the presidential oath as soon as possible. "The country should never be without a president," he declared. The only person qualified to swear in the new president was John Coolidge, who could do so in his position as a **notary public**. So at 2:47 A.M., by the soft glow of a kerosene lamp, Calvin Coolidge put his hand on the family Bible and repeated the oath after his father. He wore a blue serge jacket and a white shirt and tie for the occasion. The witnesses to this historic moment included Grace Coolidge, Congressman Dale, and the twenty-two-year-old editor of a

Springfield, Vermont, weekly newspaper, who got the news scoop of his career.

After the brief ceremony was over, Coolidge said good night to the people in the parlor and returned upstairs with Grace. The man who had just become the thirtieth president of the United States went back to sleep for several more hours. He did not seem at all overwhelmed by the sudden rush of events. As he told Grace earlier, "I think I can swing it." The understatement of that comment was characteristic of the quiet, confident man who had been shaped by his small-town New England upbringing.

Coolidge's father, John, had a great influence on his son's commitment to public service and economic thrift.

A Vermont Boyhood

John Calvin Coolidge was born on July 4, 1872, in the tiny village of Plymouth Notch, Vermont. In Coolidge's youth the village consisted of a general store, a two-room schoolhouse, a church, and seven farmhouses. Coolidge was born in the five-room house attached to the general store owned and operated at the time by his father, whom he was named after. To avoid confusion with his father, he was called Calvin or Cal from an early age. After college he dropped the name John entirely.

The Coolidges were of old Yankee stock. The first Coolidge,

also named John, arrived in Massachusetts in 1630. A later ancestor fought in the Revolutionary War. The family had lived in Plymouth Notch for four generations. John Coolidge made his living from the general store and farming, but he also pursued a second career as a public servant. He was a justice of the peace and a notary public. He went on to serve three terms in the Vermont House of Representatives and one term in the State Senate. When Calvin was three, he went with his grandfather and mother to the state capitol in Montpelier to hear his father speak in the legislature. "My father had qualities that were greater than any I possess . . . untiring industry and great tenacity of purpose . . . unnerving judgment," he wrote years later.

If he admired his father, Cal adored his mother, Victoria Josephine Moor Coolidge, a sensitive, attractive woman who loved nature and poetry. "Whatever was grand and beautiful in form and color attracted her," Coolidge wrote in his autobiography. "It seemed as though the rich green tints of the foliage and the blossoms of the flowers came for her in the springtime, and in the autumn it was for her that the mountain sides were struck with crimson and with gold." His mother's fragile health, caused in large part by tuberculosis, was

Victoria Josephine Moor Coolidge died while Coolidge was just a young boy.

Coolidge at age seven

worsened by the birth of Calvin's sister Abigail in 1875.

Young Calvin had a fair complexion, freckles, blue eyes, and bright red hair that later turned sandy. He suffered from allergies and bouts of asthma but otherwise was in good health. Like other boys his age, he spent his time in the local two-room schoolhouse when he was not at home doing the many chores farmers' children did. These included splitting wood, plowing fields, and tapping maple trees in the late winter and early spring for their valuable sap. John Coolidge used to brag that his son could tap more sap from a maple tree than any other boy his size.

The Coolidges treated their children well but did not spoil them. "Whenever the hired man or the hired girl wanted to go anywhere they were always understood to be entitled to my place in the wagon, in which case I remained at home," Coolidge noted years later. "This gave me a very early training in democratic ideas and impressed upon me very forcibly the dignity and power, if not the superiority of labor. It was all a fine atmosphere in which to raise a boy."

FATHER AND SON

John Coolidge was one of very few presidents' fathers who lived to see their son in the White House. It was a matter of great pride to both men. "I think of him just as a good and honest boy, who will do his best with any job given him," John Coolidge told reporters when his son became president. They were extremely close and kissed each other in public. The father visited his son at the White House often. He did, however, turn down the president's invitation to live there. When John Coolidge became terminally ill, the president called him daily on a direct phone line. "I wish you were here where you could have every care and everything made easy

for you," Coolidge wrote his father in 1926, "but I know you feel more content at home." John Coolidge, age eighty, died soon after, before the president could reach his side. "When I reached home, he was gone," Coolidge wrote in his autobiography. "It costs a great deal to be President." In this photo, Coolidge is sworn in as president by his father, John.

Two Tragedies

When Calvin was twelve, his mother died of tuberculosis. She was thirty-nine years old. "We laid her away in the blustering snows of March. The greatest grief that can come to a boy came to me," he wrote years later. "Life was never to seem the same again." As an adult he kept his mother's photograph on his desk and carried a lock of her hair in a locket.

The next year Coolidge graduated from the local school and was accepted at a private, live-in secondary school, the Black River Academy, 12 miles away in Ludlow. "This was one of the greatest events of my life," Coolidge later wrote about leaving for the academy. "The packing and preparation for it required more time and attention than collecting my belongings in preparation for leaving the White House. I counted the hours until it was time to go." Quiet and shy, Coolidge began at the academy as only an average student but gradually improved. Some weekends he would walk the 12 miles to his home to spend time with his father and sister, Abby.

In his last year at the academy, tragedy again struck his family. Abby suffered a burst appendix. There was no doctor in the area skilled enough to operate, and she died of an infection. She was only fourteen years old. Abby's death drew father and son closer together than ever. It was a bond that would remain strong for the rest of John Coolidge's life.

College Years

Coolidge graduated from Black River Academy in 1890 with good grades and set his sights on attending Amherst College in nearby

Amherst, Massachusetts. But on his first trip to the school, he contracted a bad cold, which contributed to his failure of the entrance exam. He returned home and took courses in the spring semester at Saint Johnsbury Academy, in northern Vermont. The president of the school recommended him to Amherst, and he was accepted in the fall of 1891. Before he left for college, his father married the local schoolteacher, Carrie Brown, who became a loving stepmother to Calvin.

Coolidge made little impression at Amherst. He was quiet, unassuming, and painfully shy. He became known as an "odd stick." "I don't seem to get ac-

This photograph was taken of Coolidge during his senior year at Amherst College.

quainted very fast," he wrote his father. He played no sports and received only average grades in his courses. That changed, however, by his junior year. Coolidge worked more diligently in his classes and gained a reputation among the other students for his dry wit and sharp sense of humor. In his senior year he was invited to join the fraternity Phi Gamma Delta and did so. He graduated **cum laude** in 1895 and was chosen by his fellow graduates to deliver a humorous tribute to the members of the senior class, known as the Grove Oration.

An Influential Teacher

At Amherst, Coolidge took a philosophy course taught by Charles Edward Garman, a professor of moral philosophy and metaphysics. Garman's influence on Coolidge, and on many other students, was profound. He taught his students to think for themselves and to come to their own conclusions about philosophy and life. He reinforced in Coolidge the importance of hard work and instilled in him a responsibility as a Christian to do good deeds in the world. When he was president, Coolidge kept *The Life and Letters of Charles E. Garman* on his bedside table and read it frequently. "To Garman was given a power which took his class up into a high mountain of spiritual life and left them alone with God," Coolidge wrote in his autobiography.

Anxious to find success in life and make his father proud of him, Coolidge took his father's advice and decided to become a lawyer. He moved to Northampton, Massachusetts, a few miles from Amherst College. It would become his permanent home for the rest of his life. At that time many young men who pursued a career in law did not go to law school but learned by working as a clerk in a law firm. Coolidge was hired for that position by the firm of John C. Hammond and Henry P. Field in September 1895. At night he studied the law and honed his writing skills. That December Coolidge was awarded a gold medal worth $150 by the Sons of the American Revolution for winning a national essay contest he had entered in his senior year of college. The title was "The Principles Fought for in the American Revolution."

Northampton—Paradise City

"[A] quiet but substantial town, with pleasant surroundings and fine old traditions," was how Coolidge described Northampton, Massachusetts. Northampton was founded in 1654 as Nonotuck. Although Calvin Coolidge is one of its most celebrated residents, a number of other famous people have made their homes there. They include the African-American evangelist and reformer Sojourner Truth; the author Lydia Maria Child, who wrote the Thanksgiving song "Over the River and Through the Woods"; and Sylvester Graham, the creator of the graham cracker. The abolitionist Frederick Douglass was a frequent visitor to Northampton, and Alexander Graham Bell, the inventor of the telephone, taught at the city's Clarke School for the Deaf in the 1870s. The famed Swedish singer and actress Jenny Lind once visited Northampton and gave it the name "Paradise City." The city celebrated its 350th anniversary in 2004.

First Steps in Politics

When Henry Field ran for mayor of Northampton as a **Republican** in the fall of 1895, Coolidge worked on his campaign. Field won, and his partner John Hammond was elected district attorney. The shy Coolidge enjoyed being part of the campaign, and found comradeship in the local political scene. His home state of Vermont was a Republican state, and Coolidge naturally felt drawn to its conservative but fair philosophy. He became active in Northampton's Republican Party, and in 1897 was named a party committeeman in his political **ward**. That same year Coolidge was admitted to the bar and soon after opened his own law practice on Main Street. Admired for his hard work and honesty, Coolidge was nominated by his party for a seat on the city council and won. The job offered no pay but gave him the opportunity to meet people who were important in the community. It was the start of one of the luckiest and most unlikely political careers in twentieth-century American politics.

FROM COUNCILMAN TO GOVERNOR

$\mathcal{A}$t first glance Calvin Coolidge would seem ill equipped to enter the rough-and-tumble world of politics. His shy, retiring nature could not have been further from the popular image of the outgoing, glad-handing politician. Yet his strengths as an administrator and faithful party worker balanced out his difficulty with relating to people. His fellow New Englanders took a liking to this typically sour-faced Yankee, with his shrewd mind and dry wit. More important, the local Republican Party leaders were impressed by his loyalty, work ethic, and skill as a lawyer. In 1900 he was voted the city's solicitor, a position he held for two years. In 1903 he was named clerk of the courts for Hampshire County, which included Northampton.

COURTSHIP AND MARRIAGE

Despite his growing success in the law and in politics, Coolidge earned a modest income and lived in a boardinghouse in the

This photograph was taken during Coolidge's time as the solicitor for the city of Northampton, Massachusetts.

Round Hill section of Northampton. One day in 1904 he was shaving in front of a window in his room, wearing only his long underwear and a straw hat on his head. Suddenly he heard a woman's laughter. He looked outside and saw an attractive young lady staring at him from the grounds of the adjoining Clarke School for the Deaf. She was watering flowers when she saw him and quickly turned away. Coolidge was embarrassed but also intrigued. He was so attracted by this pretty woman that he managed to overcome his shyness, find out who she was, and later introduce himself.

The woman was Grace Goodhue, a teacher at the Clarke School. Coolidge explained at their first meeting that he wore the straw hat each morning to press down a stubborn cowlick in

On October 4, 1905, Calvin Coolidge married Grace Goodhue.

his hair. Now Grace was intrigued, and the two, who attended the same Congregational Church, began to go to church social events together, much to the surprise of her friends. It was a classic case of opposites attracting. Grace was warmhearted, outgoing, and talkative. Coolidge recognized her strengths and was good-humored about his own weaknesses. "[H]aving taught the deaf to hear, Miss Goodhue might perhaps cause the mute to speak," a friend of Coolidge's joked.

Grace Goodhue Coolidge

Calvin Coolidge could not have found a better helpmate in his life and career than Grace Goodhue. She was born an only child on January 3, 1879, in Burlington, Vermont. Her father was a mechanical engineer, and she attended the University of Vermont. Grace graduated Phi Beta Kappa, with high academic distinction, in 1902. She was the first president's wife to have graduated from a coeducational university. Although soon after her marriage, Grace left her teaching job at the Clarke School, she retained an interest in and supported the welfare of hearing-impaired people all her life.

Grace was not the political confidante of her husband, and he never consulted her on political matters. Yet she served him well as a gracious and popular hostess both as a governor's wife and later as the First Lady of the nation. Grace's outgoing personality made her very popular with the public, and her passions ranged from baseball to theater and music. She was a devoted fan of the Washington Senators baseball team and cheered them on to their victory in the 1925 World Series. Grace Coolidge survived her husband by twenty-four years, dying at age seventy-eight on July 7, 1957, in Northampton.

But that did not appear to be the case. After the couple became engaged, Grace persuaded him to accompany her on a visit to an old college friend. "My friend was normally a talkative person," Grace recalled years later, "but our conversation upon this occasion was halting, and we received no assistance from the man [Coolidge] on the sofa. Not one word did he utter and when, at last, he could bear it no longer, he arose and said simply, with one of his best smiles, 'We'll be going now.' While he went to get the nag [horse], my nonplussed friend exclaimed, 'My lord, Grace, I'd be afraid of him!' As we drove homeward I protested: 'Now why did you act like that? She thinks that you are a perfect stick and said she'd be afraid of you.'" "She'll find I'm human," replied her fiancé.

The couple was married on October 4, 1905, at her parents' home. He was thirty-three, and she was twenty-six. They spent a short honeymoon in Montreal, Canada, and then returned to Northampton to live in half of a two-family house that they rented for $28 dollars a month.

His Honor the Mayor

In the fall of 1905 Coolidge ran for a seat on the board of education and was defeated. It was the only election he ever lost. Party leaders urged him to run for a seat in the Massachusetts House of Representatives in 1906. He did, and won with a majority of 264 votes. Coolidge served his district in Boston, the capital, for two one-year terms. He made little impression as a state legislator but earned a voting record that was slightly progressive.

Coolidge was lonely and homesick, living in a hotel room at the modest Adams House, while his wife and their first child, John, born in 1906, remained at home in Northampton. When a second son, Calvin Jr., was born in April 1908, Coolidge decided not to seek a third term and returned home to his law practice. But politics was now in his blood, and when the opportunity came to run for mayor of Northampton in 1909, he entered the race. He was thirty-nine years old and said he was running to "please my father, advance me in my profession, and enable me to be of

When the Coolidge family sat for this photo, little did they know that Calvin would become governor of Massachusetts three years later.

some public service." In the election he beat his opponent, a **Democrat** whom Coolidge identifies in his autobiography only as "a popular merchant" and "a personal friend of mine." Coolidge won by just 165 votes.

Coolidge was an active and, surprisingly, progressive-minded mayor. Some historians believe his progressive actions in his early political career were due more to his being responsive to the needs of his constituents than to any deeper political philosophy. He raised the salaries of teachers, expanded the police force and fire department, and worked to improve streets and sidewalks to make them safer. He was a popular mayor and was reelected a year later. "Of all the honors that have come to me," Coolidge later wrote, "I still cherish in a very high place the confidence of my friends and neighbors in making me their mayor."

As his second term was drawing to an end, the state senator for Northampton was about to retire. Republican leaders persuaded Coolidge to run for his seat, and he won the election in the fall of 1911. The four years Coolidge spent in the senate gave him the experience to become a political leader. Again, although a professed conservative, he pursued a largely progressive agenda. He supported women's **suffrage** and the provision of aid to

Young girls attend a suffrage meeting with placards reading "Votes for Us When We Are Women."

needy mothers. He helped pass bills that provided a minimum wage and **pensions** for woman workers. He also supported workmen's **injury compensation**, a state income tax, and the direct election by popular vote of U.S. senators. In his fourth term in the senate Coolidge was elected president of that body and worked hard to make the legislature more efficient. He disliked long speeches and meetings, and encouraged his fellow legislators to "be brief," a rule he held to in his own speeches.

GOVERNOR COOLIDGE

In 1915 Coolidge ran for the office of **lieutenant governor** on the Republican ticket with gubernatorial candidate Samuel McCall. Among the Republicans who went to Massachusetts to campaign for McCall and Coolidge was Senator Warren G. Harding of Ohio. McCall and Coolidge won, defeating the **incumbent** Democrat, Governor David Walsh. Coolidge served three terms as lieutenant governor. He gained valuable political experience heading the state's finance and pardon committees and serving on the governor's advisory board. The public came to trust and admire him, and so did his fellow Republicans. "[A]mong the clever orators, eager reformers, and shrewd politicians by whom he is surrounded, he seems to me to be the one man whose thought and work is all *constructive*," wrote the Boston department store owner Frank W. Stearns in a letter to a friend. "That is what I, in common with many others, have been looking for, that is what I believe I have found in Coolidge."

In 1918, with the support of Stearns and other leading members of the Republican Party, Coolidge ran for governor against the Democrat Richard H. Long. The campaign took place under trying circumstances. World War I, which the United States had entered in 1917, was still being fought. An epidemic of influenza prevented the Republicans from holding a state convention. While some Republicans sharply criticized the Democratic president Woodrow Wilson's handling of the war, Coolidge supported the president. This undoubtedly cost him votes. The campaign required that he travel around the state, giving speeches and meeting many more people than he had ever met before. It was a daunting challenge for the shy lawyer. It reminded him, as he later wrote, of his boyhood: "I would go into a panic if I heard strange voices in the kitchen . . . and the hardest thing in the world was to have to go through the kitchen door and give them a greeting. I'm all right with old friends, but every time I meet a stranger, I've got to go through the old kitchen door, back home, and it's not easy."

He was not the ideal candidate. When he gave a speech, he delivered it with an unpleasant nasal twang and a monotonous tone. But the people of Massachusetts looked beyond his flaws and elected him governor by a slim margin of 17,035 votes.

Coolidge ran for governor of Massachusetts as World War I raged in Europe.

As governor, Coolidge continued to pursue what people today would call a "compassionate conservatism." He backed bills that limited the workweek for women and children to forty-eight hours and increased workmen's compensation allowances. He showed an interest in preserving the environment by backing legislation that would fund new state forests and control outdoor advertising. Always looking for ways to curb government spending, Coolidge reorganized the state government to make it more efficient and less costly, reducing the number of state departments from 144 to 20. However, he also pushed for increased pay for teachers, police officers, and factory workers. Coolidge's efforts on behalf of the police to get them better pay did not succeed, and ironically, that ended up serving him well.

THE BOSTON POLICE STRIKE

The Boston city police commissioner Edwin U. Curtis was strongly opposed to the formation of unions for public servants. When a group of police officers organized a union to defend their rights under the guidance of the American Federation of Labor (AFL), Curtis suspended nineteen of the group's leaders. In response police officers threatened to go on strike.

"Understand that I do not approve of any strike," declared Governor Coolidge. "But can you blame the police for feeling as they do when they get less than a street car conductor?" On September 9, 1919, more than 1,100 officers, 75 percent of the Boston force, walked off the job. That night a crime wave swept through the city. Men boldly gambled with dice on Boston Commons. Wild youths smashed store windows with rocks and then looted the stores. Innocent citizens were stopped on the streets and robbed by criminals.

Rioters converge in Boston during the 1919 police strike.

The Boston mayor Andrew Peters called in the state militia the next day to restore order. But that night the situation turned worse. Riots broke out, and the rioters clashed with the militia. Dozens of people were injured, and two men were shot to death in South Boston. Governor Coolidge had been reluctant to get involved in what he saw as a city matter, but now he felt he had no choice but to intervene. He called out the state national guardsmen, who quickly restored order. Then Coolidge declared that the striking officers be fired. AFL leader Samuel Gompers

THE PALMER RAIDS

Only three months before the Boston police strike, a package bomb exploded on the front porch of U.S. attorney general A. Mitchell Palmer's home. The man delivering the bomb died in the explosion, and a Communist pamphlet was found near his body. Other bombs were mailed to a number of important Americans who opposed unionized labor.

Palmer quickly decided to fight back against all those he called "alien Bolsheviks." He ordered one hundred federal agents to round up and arrest suspected leftists in eighteen major cities. Four thousand men and women were arrested, many of them on the flimsiest of evidence. Palmer went even further and had anyone requesting to visit one of the arrested people detained as well, reasoning that they too must be radical communists.

Secretary of labor William B. Wilson insisted that the accused be given a fair hearing. As a result half of those arrested were released because of lack of evidence. Of those who remained in jail, six hundred were deported from the United States. None of the bombers was ever found. The "Red Scare" that led to the Palmer Raids would continue to haunt the United States throughout the 1920s.

dashed off a telegram to Coolidge, urging him to take back this order. Coolidge sent a curt message back to Gompers. "There is no right to strike against the public safety by anybody, anyplace, anytime," the telegram said.

Coolidge's words struck a chord with many Americans. People feared that the labor movement had been infiltrated by communists who opposed the private ownership of property, the American democratic system, and government by any authority other than the Communist Party. Only two years earlier Russia had undergone a violent revolution. The people overthrew the hereditary monarch, the czar, and a provisional government took power. Russian communists then seized power from the provisional government, and the Bolshevik Party (communists) took control of the country.

Newspapers across the nation put Coolidge's stance "for law and order" against the strikers on the front page. He received 70,000 supportive telegrams and letters, including one from the president of the United States, Woodrow Wilson. Overnight, the little-known governor of Massachusetts had become a national figure. Ironically, Coolidge felt his actions would be unpopular and ruin his chances of reelection. In November 1919 he was reelected by 125,101 votes. But there were greater triumphs to come.

A RELUCTANT VICE PRESIDENT

$\mathcal{T}$he 1920 Republican National Convention was held in Chicago, Illinois, in June. After eight years of the administration of Democrat Woodrow Wilson, the Republicans felt their chances of winning back the presidency were very good. Wilson had led the United States into World War I in 1917, in which the country suffered 320,518 casualties. When the war ended in victory for the United States and its allies the following year, Wilson helped organize the League of Nations, an organization dedicated to peacefully resolving international conflicts. Wilson worked hard to get the United States to join the League of Nations, but without success. The American public and many of its elected legislators were still reeling from the heavy price in lives the war had cost the nation and wanted to avoid any further foreign entanglements. It rejected membership in the League of Nations. Wilson, overcome with exhaustion, suffered a stroke in 1919 and soon left office an invalid.

The Republicans had a number of eager candidates for their presidential nomination. They included General Leonard Wood, a hero of the Spanish-American War of 1898; the California senator Hiram Johnson; and the Illinois governor Frank Lowden. The Massachusetts governor Calvin Coolidge was being touted by state delegates as a **favorite son** candidate for president. Although Coolidge didn't actively seek the nomination, he received thirty-four votes on the first ballot. This was far fewer votes than were

In their search for a vice presidential candidate, delegates at the 1920 Republican convention in Chicago nominated Calvin Coolidge.

received by Johnson and Lowden, and Coolidge's support quickly dwindled.

The balloting continued far into the night without any one candidate emerging with a majority. Finally, a small circle of powerful senators, including Massachusetts's Henry Cabot Lodge, adjourned to a room in the Blackstone Hotel. They saw it as their mission to choose a presidential candidate who would be agreeable to enough delegates to secure the nomination.

Two Dark Horses

The senators in the smoke-filled hotel room wanted a candidate who was not well known, had few political enemies, and was someone over whom they could exert their influence. They settled on Senator Warren G. Harding of Ohio. Harding looked like a president. He was tall, handsome, and genial but had an undistinguished record in his six years in the Senate. With the help of these influential and powerful politicians, Harding was nominated on the tenth ballot.

The circle of powerful senators had their handpicked choice for vice president, too. He was Senator Irvine L. Lenroot of Wisconsin. As Lenroot's name was put into nomination, a number of delegates, tired after four days at the convention and convinced Lenroot would become the nominee, left the hall. Then something unexpected happened. Judge Wallace McCamant, a delegate from Oregon, jumped up on a chair and delivered a short but passionate nominating speech for the "law and order" governor of Massachusetts, Calvin Coolidge. Suddenly Coolidge's nomination caught on in the convention hall like wildfire. Delegates vividly recalled his strong stand against the police strike in Boston. The rank-and-file delegates were also not happy with the way Harding had been foisted on them by a few powerful senators. They decided then and there that they would have their own vice presidential candidate. Much to the disappointment of Senator Lenroot and his supporters, Coolidge won the nomination on the first ballot, with 674 votes to Lenroot's 146. Senator Lodge must have been especially disappointed. Four years earlier at the Republican convention, Coolidge's name

Warren G. Harding and Calvin Coolidge meet in Washington, D.C., to plan their campaign.

had briefly been raised as a vice presidential candidate, causing Lodge to cry out, "Coolidge—my God!"

But Coolidge, who was in Boston that fateful night, had a somewhat similar reaction when he received the news by phone that he had been nominated. "You're not going to accept it, are you?" Grace Coolidge asked. "I suppose I shall have to," replied her husband.

THE VICE PRESIDENCY

"My country has in its wisdom contrived for me the most insignificant office that ever the invention of man created or his imagination can," wrote John Adams, the nation's first vice president, in a letter to his wife. Adams had good reason to be unhappy in his position. The vice presidency, as conceived by the Constitution, was mostly a ceremonial role in the new federal government. His only official duties were to preside over the U.S. Senate and oversee the counting of the electoral vote in presidential elections. Originally, the vice president was a candidate for president who received the second-highest number of votes. This made for problems when the president and vice president were from different political parties. In 1804 Congress ratified the Twelfth Amendment to the Constitution, calling for separate ballots for president and vice president. This solved one problem but created another. The vice presidency became even less important an office than before. Political parties chose a vice presidential candidate more for the votes he could bring in from his state or region than for his abilities.

But there was always the possibility that the president might die in office. In that case the vice president would succeed him as president. John Adams must have realized this when he wrote, "In this office I am nothing, but I may be everything." Adams did become president, but he did it on his own, getting elected to that office in 1796.

THE 1920 ELECTION

The presidential election of 1920 was a decisive one in American politics. Would the United States accept the role of an international power among nations, as it had been in World War I, or would it retreat from the world stage and isolate itself?

The Democratic ticket was headed by Governor James M. Cox of Ohio and his running mate, the thirty-eight-year-old assistant secretary of the navy, Franklin Delano Roosevelt. They felt that it was the nation's responsibility and destiny to play a major role on the world stage. They made speeches around the country advocating that the United States join the League of Nations to help initiate world peace and prevent another major war. Both men campaigned hard. Roosevelt traveled the country, delivering an average of ten speeches a day.

The Republican ticket campaigned less rigorously. Harding sat out most of the campaign on his front porch in Marion, Ohio, giving short speeches to reporters and passersby. His campaign slogan was a "Return to Normalcy" that would bring America back

Franklin Delano Roosevelt (right) and James M. Cox took to the streets in Dayton, Ohio, during the 1920 election.

Warren G. Harding campaigns from the front porch of his home in Marion, Ohio.

to the simpler, happier days it enjoyed before World War I. Harding largely sidestepped the question of League of Nations membership. Most Republicans feared that joining the league would lessen the authority of the United States among other nations. Coolidge campaigned more actively, although his only trip outside of New England was a brief tour of the South. The strategy for his visit was to attempt to grab some votes from the Democrats in that Democratic stronghold, the "Solid South." The South had voted Democratic since the Civil War, when the Republican Party strongly opposed the Southern institution of slavery.

The simpler, prosperous past that the Republicans harked back to appealed to a majority of Americans, and on Election Day, Harding and Coolidge won a landslide victory. They gained just over 60 percent of the popular vote and took 404 of the electoral votes, compared to 127 electoral votes for the Democrats. Franklin Roosevelt lost his first—and last—election. Twelve years later he would become the first Democratic president since Woodrow Wilson.

Silent Cal

Coolidge cut an odd figure as Harding's vice president. The new president was an easygoing, popular man with many friends. He brought many of these friends with him from Ohio and appointed some of them as aides and cabinet members. The vice president did not fit in well with this chummy group of worldly men, who liked to sit around in the White House at night, playing poker and drinking alcohol. But Harding, who liked Coolidge, gave him more authority than was given to any vice president before him. He invited Coolidge to sit in as an official member of his cabinet, a privilege given to no previous vice president. Coolidge agreed to do so but seldom spoke in cabinet meetings. Outside of giving formal speeches, he seldom spoke in public at all, despite the many state dinners and social functions he was required to attend as vice president. "Sometimes I don't know whether I'm having food or soda mints [for indigestion], I have to mix the two so often," he once joked about all the eating out he did. His refusal to make small talk earned him the nickname "Silent Cal." "If you don't say anything," Coolidge said, "you can't be called on to repeat it."

Harding's cabinet was known for its sociable manner, one that Coolidge (seated second from right) did not fit in with.

He carried this philosophy into the Senate chambers. One time, as presiding officer of the Senate, Coolidge was asked by a senator who was proadministration to allow him to speak on a particular issue. But by doing so, Coolidge knew he would displease another important senator. So to avoid any conflict, the vice president simply turned his gavel over to the first senator and left the chamber until the matter was settled.

Coolidge kept such a low profile as vice president that he often went unrecognized in Washington. Once a fire broke out in the

Though not comfortable at social events, Vice President Coolidge (second from left) was required to attend.

Willard Hotel, where he and Grace lived. As he returned to the hotel after the evacuation, Coolidge was stopped by a fire marshal. "I'm the vice president," he said, identifying himself. The marshal let him go in, but then stopped him again. "What are you vice president of?" he asked. "I am the vice president of the United States," replied Coolidge in a huff. "Come right down," said the marshal with a grin. "I thought you were vice president of the hotel."

COOLIDGE AND THE SOCIALITE

Many stories, some true and others fictitious, have been told about Coolidge's reluctance to speak. The most celebrated one involved a Washington socialite who sat next to the vice president at a dinner party. "I made a bet with a friend that I could get more than two words out of you," she told Coolidge. Before leaving the table, Coolidge gave her a wry smile and said, "You lose." Although a good story, it is probably not a true one. Historians believe Coolidge would have been too much of a gentleman to have insulted a woman in public that way.

DEATH OF A PRESIDENT

Harding was a popular president and, although he had personal flaws, he was about as honest politically as Coolidge. But he was weak-willed and a poor judge of character. Some of the friends he had placed in top positions in his administration were corrupted by the power they wielded. Secretary of the interior Albert Fall secretly leased government oil lands to developers for personal gain, including one oil field called Teapot Dome in Wyoming. Attorney general Harry Daugherty was also guilty of accepting bribes. There were other scandals as well. When Harding began to learn the truth, he felt betrayed. To escape the pressures of government and his own disillusionment, he took a transcontinental train trip to Alaska, then a U.S. territory. It was a combination goodwill and campaign trip along the

ACCIDENTAL PRESIDENTS

Five vice presidents before Coolidge had become president on the death of the president. In 1840 John Tyler assumed the presidency on the death of William Henry Harrison, who had been in office for less than a month when he died of pneumonia. Many people in government thought Tyler should be given only the title of acting president until a new president could be elected. They didn't even want him to move into the White House. Tyler, however, ignored these people and assumed the role of rightful president, creating a precedent that has been followed ever since. Nine years later Millard Fillmore succeeded Zachary Taylor as president when Taylor died in office. Andrew Johnson finished out Abraham Lincoln's second term after Lincoln's assassination in 1865. Chester Arthur and Theodore Roosevelt also took the reins of government from Presidents James Garfield and William McKinley, both victims of assassins' bullets. Most of these accidental presidents would probably have agreed with Andrew Johnson's words upon becoming president: "I feel incompetent to perform duties so important and responsible as those which have been so unexpectedly thrown upon me."

West Coast. During the journey more details of the scandals leaked out and were secretly reported to the president. Angry and distraught and suffering from a bout of what his physician believed was acute indigestion, Harding stopped for several days in San Francisco on his return trip. He was resting in bed at the Palace Hotel on the evening of August 2, 1923, as his wife read him a magazine article. Without warning, Harding suffered a massive stroke and died.

Coolidge, vacationing in Vermont at his father's home, was sworn in as president the next morning. The man who never wanted to be vice president was now saddled with the toughest job of all.

The death of Warren G. Harding is announced on the front page of the August 3, 1923, New York Times.

COOLIDGE PROSPERITY

Four

On December 6, 1923, the new president delivered his first message to Congress, the first speech of its kind to be broadcast over the radio. Coolidge emphasized the Republican ideas that Harding had upheld. American business should be encouraged to grow by cutting taxes. The federal government should keep a tight rein on spending, making more cuts in the military than those initiated by Harding. The United States should isolate itself from the problems of Europe to avoid getting into another war. Although President Coolidge did not support the League of Nations, he did support the United States joining the World Court, an international body of judges that met in the Hague in the Netherlands to resolve problems between countries. Congress would not agree to join, however, without amendments to its membership. The World Court refused to meet these amendments, and Coolidge gave up the fight. The United States would not become part of an international peacekeeping organization until the formation of the United Nations in 1945.

DEALING WITH SCANDAL

The transition from the Harding to the Coolidge administration seemed to be a smooth one. Then, in January 1924, the so-called Teapot Dome scandal, the illegal issuance of government oil leases, became public. Until then, Harding had been seen by many Americans as a good, even a great, president. With the exposure

42

This political cartoon satirizes the Teapot Dome scandal with political officials trying to outpace the scandal.

of this scandal and others in his administration, that image was shattered forever. Harding's presidency has since been viewed as one of the most corrupt in American history, and most historians judge Harding as one of our weakest presidents.

As the unseemly details of the Harding scandals came out in the press, Coolidge was as shocked and disillusioned as the rest of the country. "Let the guilty be punished," he declared in a press conference. One by one, those accused of corruption left the administration or were forced out. Secretary of the navy Edwin Denby, who had secretly transferred oil leases controlled by the navy to the Department of the Interior, resigned. Secretary of the interior Albert Fall, the central figure in Teapot Dome, went on trial for bribery and received a one-year prison sentence. Attorney general Daugherty hung on for a while, protesting his innocence, but when he refused to hand over private papers to a Senate investigation committee, Coolidge forced him to resign. Daugherty was later tried for bribery twice, but neither time was he convicted.

Coolidge's cabinet was comprised of only those who were untouched by the scandals during the Harding administration.

Coolidge kept only those members of Harding's cabinet who were untouched by the scandals, including commerce secretary Herbert Hoover, secretary of the treasury Andrew W. Mellon, and secretary of state Charles E. Hughes. He replaced the others with men of impeccable character. Harlan F. Stone became the new attorney general. A year later Coolidge appointed him to the Supreme Court. Curtis D. Wilbur, the chief justice of the California Supreme Court, replaced Denby as secretary of the navy. Coolidge replaced William Burns, head of the Federal Bureau of Investigation, who was implicated in the scandals, with the bureau's deputy head, J. Edgar Hoover. The scandals eventually faded, leaving no stain on the Coolidge administration.

PRESIDING OVER AMERICA'S BUSINESS

While a relatively active and progressive legislator and governor, Coolidge saw his job as president in a different light. He viewed the presidency as largely a caretaker position. He believed that a reluctance to act in this high office was a virtue that would help avoid problems. "If you see ten troubles coming down the road you can be sure that nine will run into the ditch before they reach you and you have to battle with only one of them," he said. Coolidge's do-nothing attitude seemed to fit the mood of the nation. As one person put it, the country "wanted nothing done and he [Coolidge] done it."

"The chief business of America is business," Coolidge declared in a January 1925 speech to the American Society of Newspaper Editors. And he meant it. He felt that the government should stay out of business's way and allow it to grow and flourish without restraints or regulations. It was Coolidge's

WHAT A FRIEND WE HAVE IN COOLIDGE!

This 1924 political cartoon draws upon the popularity of President Coolidge's nonrestrictive policies with American businesses.

fervent belief, along with that of many other people at the time, that big business, if left alone, would provide employment and prosperity for all Americans. To make it easier for businesses to expand, Coolidge's secretary of the treasury Mellon, the third-richest man in America, cut taxes to the rich twice through the Revenue Acts of 1924 and 1926. Antimonopoly laws were not strictly enforced during the Coolidge administration. To prevent foreign manufacturers from competing with American businesses, Coolidge supported high tariffs on imported goods.

But what was good for business was not necessarily good for other sectors of the economy. American farmers were increasing their harvests through the use of better farming methods and new technology. But this surplus of crops caused prices to drop, and farmers desperately needed to find new markets for their goods abroad. High tariffs on exports made the surplus too costly for foreign countries to buy. Congress passed a bill that would enable the federal government to buy the surplus from the farmers and sell it abroad, but Coolidge vetoed the bill twice, and it never passed. The farmers, Coolidge felt, should take care of their own problems without government assistance.

Farmers with an abundance of crops suffered from high tariffs on exports and low crop prices.

Although he paid them honor for their sacrifices in speeches, Coolidge showed little empathy for the veterans of World War I. Many veterans who returned home were unable to find jobs. The Senate's **Bonus Bill**, passed by Congress in 1923, would help veterans get back on their feet by paying them about $1,000 per man for their service over a period of twenty years. The total cost of the Bonus Bill was $3.5 billion. Coolidge was against such a large expenditure and vetoed it. Congress passed the Bonus Bill again by a two-thirds majority in both houses, overriding the president's veto. All in all, Coolidge exercised his presidential veto fifty times during his presidency. Harding used his veto only six times. If Coolidge was reluctant to say yes to anything, he had no trouble saying no, especially when it came to spending the government's money.

THE IMMIGRATION BILL OF 1924

Coolidge and Congress were more in tune with each other on the issue of immigration. Fearing that an influx of poor and uneducated immigrants from southern and eastern Europe would change American society for the worse, Congress passed the Immigration Bill of May 1924. The law declared that only 2 percent of the population of each nationality already settled in the

The Immigration Bill of 1924 limited the number of people who could enter the United States.

COOLIDGE AND THE KLAN

The white supremacist organization Ku Klux Klan, formed by white Southerners after the Civil War, had largely died out by the 1870s. But it was revived in 1915 in Georgia, and by the early 1920s Klan membership nationwide peaked at five million. The new Klan was opposed to the growing number of non–northern European immigrants and was also against African Americans, Catholics, and Jews. The Klan used its political power to help elect U.S. representatives and senators who were sympathetic to Klan views or who, in some cases, were Klan members themselves.

(continued)

Coolidge did not support the Klan or its racist agenda, but he did not speak out strongly against it, either. When 40,000 Klan members dressed in white robes marched in front of the White House in 1925, Coolidge was conveniently on vacation in Massachusetts.

Coolidge had a moderately good record on race relations for the time and a better record than those of his five predecessors in office. He officially supported antilynching legislation but took no strong stand for the betterment of African Americans. In his 1923 State of the Union address he called racial problems "to a large extent local problems which must be worked out by the mutual forbearance and human kindness of each community."

United States in 1890 could enter the country. Since there were few southern and eastern Europeans in the United States back in that year, it severely limited the number of new immigrants coming from any areas except northwestern Europe. Japanese immigrants were completely excluded. Secretary of state Hughes wanted the Japanese exclusion dropped from the bill, fearing it would seriously harm U.S.–Japanese relations. Coolidge supported him, but when Congress would not drop the exclusion, Coolidge caved in and signed the bill anyway.

"KEEPING COOL WITH COOLIDGE"

When the Republican delegates convened at their national convention in Cleveland, Ohio, in June 1924, it was clear that Coolidge was the first choice for his party's nomination for

president. Republicans were grateful for his straightforward handling of the Harding scandals and his honesty, which reflected
well on the party. As chief Supreme Court justice William Taft
put it, "the Republican Party has no chance without him."

Coolidge was nominated on the first ballot with 1,065 out of
1,109 votes. He wanted Senator William Borah of Idaho as his
running mate, but Borah refused. Harding's budget director,
Charles G. Dawes, ended up being nominated for vice president.

Two weeks later in New York City, the Democrats met to
select their presidential candidate. The Harding scandals should
have given the Democrats an edge in winning the White House,
but they could not unite behind one candidate. Seventeen names
were placed in nomination, and ballot after ballot failed to produce a
clear winner. Finally a compromise candidate, the Wall Street
lawyer and former congressman John W. Davis, from West Virginia,
was chosen on a record-breaking 103rd ballot. Nebraska governor
Charles W. Bryan was picked as his running mate.

Davis's conservative policies dismayed many liberal Democrats, so they formed their own party, the Progressive Party.
They nominated Senator Robert M. La Follette of Wisconsin as
their presidential candidate.

The Republicans' campaign slogan was "Keep Cool with
Coolidge," and nothing the opposition could do could heat up the
campaign. Coolidge himself did little active campaigning, leaving
that job to other Republicans.

A Death in the Family

Amid all the hubbub of the campaign, tragedy struck the First
Family. One day in June their son Calvin Jr. was playing tennis
with his older brother on the White House lawn. He played in

CHARLES G. DAWES, VICE PRESIDENT

Charles Dawes brought a wealth of experience and ability to the vice presidency. A native of Ohio, Dawes was a banker and a lawyer before he entered politics and became a campaign manager in Illinois for William McKinley's 1896 presidential campaign. After McKinley became president, he appointed Dawes comptroller of the currency. During World War I Dawes served as chief purchasing agent for the United States. Harding later appointed him first director of the Bureau of the Budget in 1921. Dawes's work chairing the Reparations Commission resulted in the creation of the Dawes Plan to help restore the economy of the defeated Germans after the war. For this work he shared the 1925 Nobel Peace Prize with Englishman Sir Austen Chamberlain. When his term as vice president ended, Dawes served as ambassador to Britain under President Herbert Hoover. Dawes was also an accomplished musician, a published diarist, and an amateur composer. One of his compositions became the melody for the hit pop song "It's All in the Game" in 1951, the year that he died at age eighty-five.

shoes but wore no socks and got a toe blister. The blister quickly became infected, and the boy developed blood poisoning. Today, a dose of antibiotics would have easily cured the infection, but they had not yet been discovered. As his condition worsened, Calvin Jr. was hospitalized at Walter Reed Hospital. He died there on July 7, 1924, at age sixteen. The president was grief stricken. "His face had the bleak desolation of cold November rain beating on gray Vermont granite," was how one friend described him in those terrible days.

This political cartoon by Rollin Kirby satirizes President Coolidge's inactivity during the 1924 presidential campaign.

"In his suffering, he [Calvin Jr.] was asking me to make him well. I could not," Coolidge wrote years later in his autobiography. "When he went the power and the glory of the Presidency went with him."

While the family mourned, the campaign continued. The Progressives and Democrats did all they could to attack the president's record on social and economic issues, but it made little difference. Americans were satisfied with the country's general prosperity, and they attributed that in large part to Coolidge's "hands-off" policies. On Election Day Coolidge and Dawes won 56 percent of the popular vote, a total of 15,725,106 votes, and

A 1924 Calvin Coolidge and Charles Dawes election campaign poster

382 electoral votes. Davis won 8,385,586 votes and 136 electoral votes, while La Follette ended up with 4,800,000 votes and 13 electoral votes. Silent Cal, the quiet president, had become only the second vice president to reach the presidency on his successor's death to win a full term in his own right.

A Term of His Own

On March 4, 1925, Calvin Coolidge was inaugurated president in his own right by chief justice and former president William Howard Taft. It was the first time that a former president administrated the presidential oath of office at an inauguration. In his inaugural address Coolidge spoke of offering financial relief to postwar Europe but also made it clear that "we [are] determined not to become implicated in the political controversies of the Old World." He saved his greatest passion for discussing the continued reduction of taxes and the tightening of government expenditures. "I favor the policy of economy, not because I wish to save money, but because I wish to save people," he said. "Every dollar that we carelessly waste means that their [each American's] life will be so much the more meager. . . . Economy is idealism in its most practical form." Coolidge called all unnecessary taxes "a species of legalized larceny." He declared that the United States had reached "a state of contentment seldom before seen." And the president was determined to do as little as possible to upset that contented state.

Foreign Affairs

According to Theodore Roosevelt's secretary of state Elihu Root, Coolidge "did not have an international hair on his head." This proved to be not quite accurate. It is true that Coolidge largely ignored Europe and its postwar problems. He refused to

William Howard Taft administers the oath at the 1925 inauguration of Calvin Coolidge.

recognize the new Soviet Union, the former nation of Russia and the territories it claimed. But he did take a genuine interest in, as he said in his inaugural address, "some of the small countries of the Western Hemisphere." He was especially concerned with Mexico, the United States' immediate neighbor to the south. Mexico had only emerged a few years earlier from a decade-long revolution that left it weak and exhausted. Coolidge appointed the banker and former Amherst classmate Dwight W. Morrow as ambassador to Mexico. It was one of his best appointments. Morrow got along well with the Mexicans, treated them with respect, and greatly improved relations between the two countries.

While Mexico was stable, there was social unrest in several Central American countries during Coolidge's second term, much of it caused by American interference in their affairs. Honduras was largely run by U.S. fruit companies, which controlled the country's main crop—bananas. The derogatory term "banana republic" was originally used to describe Honduras. When rebels rose up against the American-influenced government in 1924, Coolidge sent in U.S. marines to restore order and protect American interests. The following year he sent the marines into Panama, whose people were protesting American control of the Panama Canal, which had been completed in 1914. U.S. marines had occupied a third Central American country, Nicaragua, almost continually since 1912 in order to protect U.S. banks and their employees. The banks had loaned Nicaragua money and remained in control of the country's finances until the debt was paid. Coolidge sent in more troops to settle the unrest, and they remained there until 1933. Coolidge's paternal policy toward Latin America in general would be reinforced by later administrations.

In January 1928 Coolidge visited Havana, Cuba, with his wife to deliver the keynote address at the Sixth Annual International Conference of American States. Other than his brief honeymoon in Canada, it was the only time Coolidge traveled outside the United States.

Coolidge's other major achievement in foreign affairs was the Kellogg-Briand Pact. Former Minnesota senator Frank Kellogg

U.S. forces enter Nicaragua in an effort to protect the banks there.

replaced Charles Evan Hughes as secretary of state in Coolidge's second term. Kellogg worked with the French premier Aristide Briand to draw up an agreement to settle international disputes peacefully, without bloodshed. Fifteen nations signed the Kellogg-Briand Pact on August 27, 1928, in Paris, France. Eventually forty-seven other nations signed it. For Coolidge it held "a greater hope for peaceful relations than was ever before given to the world." Kellogg won the Nobel Peace Prize in 1929 for his efforts. Unfortunately, the Kellogg-Briand Pact, for all its good intentions, proved unworkable. There was no way to enforce it

President Coolidge looks on as Frank Kellogg signs the Kellogg-Briand Pact.

and stop aggressive acts toward other countries. Such emerging dictators as Italy's Benito Mussolini in the 1920s and Germany's Adolf Hitler in the 1930s simply disregarded the pact in their lust for power.

THE ROARING TWENTIES

The economic prosperity that the United States enjoyed in the postwar 1920s led many Americans, particularly those living in large cities, to enjoy life more than ever before. One way they enjoyed it was by drinking alcohol. The Volstead Act of 1919 had

This movie still from the 1920s depicts the spirit of the times.

outlawed the sale of alcoholic beverages in the United States, but that did not stop organized criminal gangs from manufacturing and selling it to otherwise law-abiding citizens. Young, fashionable, fun-loving women called flappers and their boyfriends frequented secret, illegal clubs called speakeasies, where they could drink alcohol and dance the Charleston and other new dances to bands playing a new rhythmic music called jazz. Meanwhile, the gangsters who sold the liquor grew rich and powerful, setting off a crime wave of a scale that America had never seen before.

BOOTLEGGERS AND BATHTUB GIN

It was the illegal sale and consumption of alcohol that made the "Roaring Twenties" roar. In Chicago alone there were 10,000 speakeasies, all of them eventually controlled by the number-one crime czar in the country, Al Capone. Capone himself recognized the hypocrisy of the Prohibition laws broken readily by millions of Americans. "When I sell liquor it's bootlegging," Capone said. "When my patrons serve it on silver trays on Lake Shore Drive, it's hospitality." But many ordinary citizens were making their own "hooch," or liquor. In towns and cities

(continued)

enterprising individuals set up stills to make alcohol in their kitchens, basements, or backyards. Bathtubs were filled with homemade gin that people bottled and sold to friends and strangers alike. Many of these brews, both homemade and manufactured in gang-run factories, were of poor quality. Chicago's infamous Yack Yack Bourbon, for instance, contained generous doses of burnt sugar and iodine. For those who could afford it, premium imported liquor could be bought from rumrunner Bill McCoy, who smuggled it in from the Bahamas in the Caribbean. His happy customers called his rum "the Real McCoy."

The quiet, plain-living Coolidge seemed out of step with the times. But this did not seem to bother most Americans. "[I]n the White House they have installed a frugal little man who in his personal life is the very antithesis [opposite] of the flamboyant ideal that everybody is frantically pursuing," wrote newspaper columnist Walter Lippmann in 1926. "At a time when Puritanism as a way of life is at its lowest ebb among the people, the people are delighted with a Puritan as their national symbol."

Of course, not every American was living the high life in the Roaring Twenties. Millions of average Americans in small towns and rural areas looked on the shifting values in American society with disapproval. They took consolation in their respectable, straitlaced Yankee president. Coolidge was one of them.

Social Life in the White House

The president did not drink (although he did not strenuously enforce Prohibition), rarely danced, and was usually in bed by ten o'clock. While attending a performance of the hit musical *Animal Crackers*, starring the comedy team the Marx brothers, Coolidge was addressed from the stage by Groucho Marx, who ad-libbed, "Isn't it past your bedtime, Calvin?" No president enjoyed his sleep as much as Coolidge did. He averaged eleven hours of sleep a day and took a customary nap after lunch that lasted up to two hours. "Nero fiddled while Rome burned," wrote the author and humorist H. L. Mencken, "but Coolidge only snores."

Calvin Coolidge's conservative demeanor was out of step with the raucous behavior of the mid-1920s.

Coolidge had no interest in sports or athletics. When asked how he got his exercise, he replied, "Having my picture taken." Coolidge's only concession to exercise was having a mechanical horse installed in the White House, which he would sometimes ride like a cowboy, whooping loudly. He also liked to fish on summer vacations, usually dressed in a jacket and tie and hat, and enjoyed cruising on the presidential yacht, the *Mayflower*, on Sunday afternoons. He loved watching movies (mostly silent ones) with Grace in the White House but had to be dragged by her to watch the Washington Senators baseball team play. During a tie game in the 1925 World Series, Coolidge got up to leave. Grace pleaded with him to stay. He grudgingly agreed and watched the Senators go on to win the game.

President Coolidge tosses out the first ball at a 1925 Washington Senators game.

One surprising pastime that Coolidge relished was playing practical jokes on the White House staff. "Do you know I've never really grown up," he once confided to Frank Stearns. He would sometimes push all the buttons on his desk just to see his aides come scurrying in. Even his favorite Secret Serviceman, Edmund W. Starling, who took daily walks with him, could be the butt of his jokes. "When he was satisfied that I was waiting he would dress and come downstairs," Starling recalled in a memoir. "Sometimes he would tell the elevator operator to take him to the bottom. Then he would try to sneak out the East or the West entrance, just to fool me. Everyone on the staff cooperated with me and tipped me off, so I was always able to catch him."

THE PRESIDENT'S PETS

Coolidge may have been shy and distant around most people, but he got along very well with animals. "Any man who does not like dogs and want them about, does not deserve to be in the White House," he once said. No First Family had more pets than the Coolidges did. They had twelve dogs, seven birds, three cats, and two raccoons. The raccoons were among the president's favorites. One of them, named Rebecca, was Grace's pet. A favorite Coolidge dog was a white collie named Rob Roy (right). One time Rob Roy sat looking intently at a senator who had joined Coolidge for breakfast at the White House. "Senator," said the president, looking down at the dog, "I think he wants your sausage." And Rob Roy got it.

THE FIRST MEDIA PRESIDENT

Coolidge came to the White House at a time when modern communications technology was bursting onto the national scene. Commercial radio was entering the homes of millions of

Americans. Movies had become a popular form of entertainment. Weekly newsreel films allowed Americans to see breaking news events as well as read about them in the newspapers. Coolidge was the first president to understand and make effective use of modern media. This may seem an unlikely achievement for a man who was so acutely shy and quiet. But the shrewd Yankee he was, Coolidge saw the advantages of using the media to polish his public image.

Because real news was hard to come by in a decade that was untroubled by war or major crises, the "photo op" filled many a page of the daily newspapers. Coolidge was always ready and willing to oblige photographers. He may be the most photographed president of the twentieth century, posing for photographers in every possible circumstance and wearing every kind of clothing. He dressed up in jeans and posed while doing chores at his family farm in Vermont. He threw out baseballs, albeit awkwardly, at ball games, and even put on skis with his wife on a snowless White House lawn. In one of his most famous—and funniest—photos, Coolidge dressed up in a Native-American warbonnet and posed with a visiting delegation of Native-American chiefs.

Once, when he dressed up as a cowboy in an outfit given to him while vacationing in South Dakota's Black Hills, friends asked the president why he agreed to be photographed wearing it. "The people here have sent me this costume, and they wouldn't have sent it unless they expected me to put it on," Coolidge replied. "Why shouldn't I have my picture taken with it on to please them?" "It's making people laugh," said his friends. "Well, it's good for people to laugh," said the president.

In April 1925 Coolidge became one of the first Americans to appear in a talking film. The "phonofilm," by inventor Lee

De Forest, was shown at a New York Friars Club dinner and showed the president giving a short talk on the silver screen.

President Roosevelt became famous in the 1930s for his radio "fireside chats" in which he talked directly to the American people, but Coolidge spoke on the radio just as frequently a decade before Roosevelt. He also made the presidential press conference an institution. In his sixty-seven months in office, Coolidge held 520 press conferences, an aver-

President Coolidge poses with a Sioux war bonnet, presented to him by Henry Standing Bear.

age of eight per month. Although he could be a man of few words on many occasions, he was often talkative in these press conferences when he had something on his mind.

THE SPIRALING STOCK MARKET

As American business grew and prospered, so did the **stock** market. Volume on the New York Stock Exchange grew from 227 million shares in 1920 to 920 million by 1928. For the first time in history, average middle-class people were investing in stocks with the hopes of growing rich, a dream that appeared within their grasp. "I am firm in my belief," said the industrialist John Raskob, "that anyone not only can be rich, but ought to be."

THE RISE OF RADIO

"I am very fortunate that I came in with the radio," Coolidge once said. "I can't make an engaging, rousing, or oratorical speech to a crowd . . . but I have a good radio voice, and now I can get my messages across to them without acquainting them with my lack of oratorical ability."

The first radio broadcast was made in 1906, but it wasn't until 1920 that the first commercial radio station, KDKA in Pittsburgh, opened for business. Its initial broadcast on November 2 was the announcement of the presidential election returns in the Harding-Cox race. Four years later there were nearly six hundred commercial radio stations in the

nation. In 1925 Americans bought 1.5 million radios, and the listening audience numbered fifty million. The following year, the first national radio network, the National Broadcasting Company, was founded by the Radio Corporation of America. Listeners were entertained at home by such early programming as farm news, live orchestral music, and educational lectures of all kinds. Comedy shows, dramas, and adventure shows were quick to follow and soon dominated the programming schedule. By the time Calvin Coolidge left office in 1929, radio was the number-one source of news and entertainment in America.

People who could not afford the stock prices could buy stocks on **margin**. This required them to pay only 10 percent of the price of the stock, while a broker put up the rest of the money. Many investors grew reckless and borrowed money to buy more and more stocks. This kind of **speculation** was seen by some economists as dangerous. They believed that the entire stock market, built largely on credit and speculation, could one day collapse like a house of cards. There is evidence that Coolidge may have believed their warnings, but if so, he refused to act on them. When asked to regulate the New York Stock Exchange to help stop spiraling speculation, Coolidge replied that that was the job of the state government of New York and not the federal government. He himself was an old-fashioned saver who put most of his money in the bank. A miser when it came to spending, Coolidge may have been the first—and last—president who actually saved money from his salary.

Coolidge and "Lucky Lindy"

At 7:52 A.M. on May 20, 1927, Charles A. Lindbergh, a pilot who carried mail, took off from Roosevelt Field, near New York City. Just 33.5 hours later, he landed his small plane, the *Spirit of St. Louis*, at Le Bourget Field, near Paris. He was greeted by thousands of cheering French people. Lindbergh had become the first pilot to make a solo, nonstop flight across the Atlantic Ocean and was now an international hero.

On his return to America, Lindbergh was whisked to Washington, where he met with President Coolidge. A parade in his honor marched to the Washington Monument, and Coolidge gave a speech to a crowd of 300,000 people on the Washington Mall. The president praised "this

genial, modest American youth . . . driven by an unconquerable will and inspired by the imagination and the spirit of his Viking ancestors." He promoted Lindbergh to the rank of colonel in the Army Reserve Corps and awarded him the Distinguished Flying Cross.

That day at a presidential lunch, "Lucky Lindy," as he was nicknamed, met Dwight Morrow, who was preparing to leave for his job as ambassador to Mexico. The two became good friends, and Lindbergh would later marry Morrow's daughter Anne.

A SURPRISE ANNOUNCEMENT

Coolidge had had a successful, if largely uneventful, term as president, and many political pundits predicted that he would run for a second full term in 1928. On August 2, 1927, the president held a press conference in Rapid City, in the Black Hills of South Dakota, where he was on summer vacation. While puzzled reporters looked on, Coolidge handed each of them a slip of paper on which were written the words "I do not choose to run for President in 1928." Everyone was taken by surprise by his announcement.

Characteristically, Coolidge gave no reason for his decision not to run again. He facetiously told one persistent reporter it was "because there's no chance for advancement." Later, in his autobiography, Coolidge indicated that if elected again, he would be breaking with tradition by serving for more than eight years. But at the time, there was much speculation about why he would not run. Some people in his inner circle believed he was tired and worn out. Others said he was stepping down in consideration for his wife, who had her own health problems. Still others claimed that the death of Coolidge's son had taken the joy out of the presidency for him. And a few said that Coolidge was not running because he saw the bubble of prosperity that had lasted seven long years bursting at last. Or as Grace Coolidge put it, "Poppa says there's going to be a **depression**."

FINAL YEARS

*H*erbert Hoover, Coolidge's secretary of commerce, won the Republican presidential nomination at the party convention in June 1928. While Coolidge publicly supported Hoover's candidacy, privately he disliked the man. While a member of Coolidge's cabinet, Hoover had tried to interfere with policy outside of his role as commerce secretary. "That man has offered me unsolicited advice for six years, all of it bad!" Coolidge had said of Hoover back in 1928. He played no part in the election campaign.

A NEW PRESIDENT

Hoover's Democratic opponent was the New York governor Al Smith, the first Catholic to run on a major party ticket for president. Although Smith insisted that his religion would not influence his actions as president, prejudice against Catholics hurt his candidacy. Continued national prosperity made most voters stick with the Republicans, and on Election Day, 1928, Hoover won easily.

Coolidge attended Hoover's inauguration on March 4, 1929. His advice to the new president was to keep his mouth shut as much as possible. "You have to stand, every day, three or four hours of visitors," Coolidge told him. "Nine-tenths of them want something they ought not to have. If you keep dead-still they will run down in three or four minutes. If you even cough or smile they will start up all over again."

Right after the inauguration Coolidge and Grace returned home by train to Northampton. Coolidge would return to the

Calvin Coolidge (back left) and Herbert Hoover on their way to Hoover's inauguration.

White House only once more, at Hoover's invitation, to witness the official signing of the Kellogg-Briand Pact in July. The Coolidges moved back into the old two-family house on Massasoit Street that they had first rented years before. The former president reopened his law office but did not practice law. He accepted a position with New York Life Insurance but spent most of his first year in retirement writing his autobiography, published in installments in magazines and then as a book in 1930. Coolidge also penned magazine articles and wrote a regular newspaper column, "Thinking Things Over With Calvin Coolidge," for the McClure newspaper chain. In his column he expressed his views

Calvin Coolidge, Author

While today's scholars rank him rather low as a president, Coolidge's rank as a presidential writer is considerably higher. Richard Norton Smith, presidential historian and director of several presidential libraries, called Coolidge's autobiography "one of the most revealing of presidential memoirs." He praised the lyricism of Coolidge's writing on his Vermont childhood and his expressive sense of loss at the death of loved ones, including his son Calvin Jr.

According to his wife, Coolidge wrote many of his own speeches. His speeches made while governor of Massachusetts were collected into a book, *Have Faith in Massachusetts*, that was distributed to every delegate at the 1920 Republican presidential convention. The book may have helped him gain the vice presidential nomination. Unfortunately, Coolidge destroyed most of his presidential papers when he left the White House. Some of his letters and other documents survive and can be found at the Forbes Library in Northampton, the Vermont Historical Society, and the Library of Congress in Washington, D.C.

Hundreds wait in an unemployment line in hopes of finding a job.

on a number of issues of the day. He was paid nearly $200,000 for the column but stopped writing it after a year because it took too much time and energy.

CRASH AND DEPRESSION

"I have no fears for the future of our country," President Hoover declared in his inaugural address on March 4, 1929. "It is bright with hope." But less than eight months later, that hope, built on the prosperity of the past decade, was shattered. In several disruptive sessions the New York Stock Exchange crashed, and almost overnight many of the 1.5 million Americans who were invested in it lost all their money. The crash sent the economy reeling. By November three million Americans were out of work. Banks shut down, and factories closed their doors. The Great Depression, the longest in American history, would last nearly a decade.

Coolidge must have wondered what he could have done as president to have prevented the Depression, or at least lessened its impact on American society. He had little sympathy or advice for Hoover, who took almost no immediate action to stem the tide. Coolidge was probably as bewildered by the Depression as the new president was.

Wall Street's Two Blackest Days

Thursday, October 24, 1929, began as just another day on the floor of the New York Stock Exchange on New York City's Wall Street. By 11 A.M., however, things were not going well. The number of orders to sell stocks was greater than the number of orders to buy them. Panic set in, and sellers on the floor were in a frenzy to sell off stocks before their value dropped to zero. The selling became so fast and frantic that the stock ticker that printed out results could not keep up with it. At 1:30 P.M. a group of bankers sent the exchange vice president Richard Whitney onto the floor with 20 million dollars to purchase stocks. This steadied the market again, but only for a brief time.

On the following Tuesday, October 29, the Dow Jones Industrial Average, an index showing the closing prices on a number of stocks, fell forty points as people rushed to sell off stocks that were rapidly losing their value. By the end of "Black Tuesday" nearly $15 billion in market value was gone. That amount would double in less than a month. The spiraling stock market had gone into free fall, and a national depression was about to set in.

The 1932 Election

In the spring of 1930 the Coolidges moved from Massasoit Street, where the prying eyes of neighbors and curiosity seekers had made them uncomfortable, to a twelve-room house called the Beeches. They could relax and enjoy their privacy on the estate's 9 acres.

Coolidge came out of retirement in 1932 to speak at a rally in New York City's Madison Square Garden, supporting Hoover's reelection campaign. He was well received by the crowd. Later, having lunch with the theatrical producer Otis Skinner and his wife, Mrs. Skinner told him, "Oh, Mr. Coolidge, I wish it were you that we were to vote for in November! It would be the end of this horrible depression." "It would be the beginning of mine," replied the former president with a twinkle in his eye.

When November came, Hoover lost the election to the Democratic presidential nominee Franklin Delano Roosevelt, the governor of New York. Voters were tired of Hoover's feeble efforts to end the Depression and were impressed by Roosevelt's willingness to try new things in order to set the country on the road to economic recovery. Roosevelt's activism as president would stand in sharp contrast to Coolidge's "leave things alone" philosophy. The Depression would continue to make life difficult for years to come, but Roosevelt's positive spirit, energy, and wide-ranging social programs would bring hope and gradual recovery.

LAST DAYS

Back in Northampton, Coolidge, age sixty, was not a well man. In addition to his chronic asthma, he suffered from bronchitis and indigestion. Coolidge confided in a friend that "I feel I no longer fit in with these times." On New Year's Day, 1933, he told another friend, "I am too old for my years. . . . I suppose the carrying of the responsibility takes its toll. . . . I am all burned out."

On the morning of January 5, Coolidge went to his downtown office to read his mail but left early, not feeling well. He puttered around the house for a few hours and then went upstairs to shave before joining his wife for lunch. An hour later Grace

Friends and family gather at the burial of President Calvin Coolidge in Plymouth Notch, Vermont.

Coolidge found him sprawled across the bathroom floor, dead from a massive heart attack.

President Hoover declared a thirty-day period of national mourning at Coolidge's death. Thousands of people attended the memorial service in Northampton. In his eulogy Hoover said, "Any summation of Mr. Coolidge's service to the country must conclude that America is a better place for his having lived in it." Calvin Coolidge was buried in Plymouth Notch in the family plot, alongside his son and his father. His will was short and sweet: "Not unmindful of my son John, I give all my estate, both real and personal, to my wife, Grace Coolidge, in fee simple."

John Coolidge—Presidential Son

John Coolidge was only seventeen when his family left the White House. He later went into business and married the daughter of the governor of Connecticut. Unlike many presidents' sons, he never entered the political arena. "I saw enough politics in my family and in my wife's family and I just got disenchanted with it I guess," he said in an interview in 1984. A conservative Republican, Coolidge defended his father's presidential record all his life. He complained that modern historians never gave him credit for the Kellogg-Briand Pact or his three tax cuts. "[They were] not only for the wealthy, but for everyone," he said. "Some low income people didn't have to pay anything." John Coolidge, who continued to live in his father's home village of Plymouth Notch, died in 2000.

Legacy

In the ranking of presidents most historians today place Coolidge in the lower third. As a man he had many admirable qualities, but as a president he lacked leadership. While it is true that Congress at that time was generally a stronger, more influential branch of government than the executive branch, Coolidge did little to maximize what power he had. The "bully pulpit" that Theodore Roosevelt, another vice president who rose to the presidency, used to lead the country was not for Coolidge. He was content to sit and let the machine of government run, with little input from him. His tightfistedness with federal money saved the country a billion dollars in debt a year but was devastating for American farmers and other working people. According to a Brookings Institution report in 1928, more than half of American families remained near or below the poverty level from 1923 to 1929. Coolidge's failure to put restraints on business and industry or to regulate the stock market certainly contributed to the market crash, although it would be unfair to blame the Great Depression solely on him. "The administration took the narrow interest of business groups to be the national interests, and the result was catastrophe," wrote the historian William Leuchtenberg.

Coolidge's achievements in foreign affairs were more positive but were marred by his paternalistic policy toward Latin America and the ineffectiveness of the Kellogg-Briand Pact.

Yet Coolidge had his strengths. He brought honesty and integrity to the White House at a time when the Harding scandals had left the presidency in shambles. He was popular with the public, endearing in his eccentricities, honest, and a pioneer in his masterful, if understated, use of the media, which subsequent presidents have emulated. A model of fiscal responsibility, he was the last president to substantially reduce the national debt until Bill Clinton. Among Coolidge's greatest admirers was another conservative Republican, President Ronald Reagan, who hung a portrait of the thirtieth president in the Cabinet Room. He called Coolidge "one of our most underrated presidents. . . . He served his country well and accomplished much." While recovering in the hospital from cancer surgery in 1985, Reagan was seen reading a book about Coolidge.

Another present-day Coolidge admirer is the political columnist Robert Novak. "[H]is combined personal integrity, faith in the market system and concern for the ordinary citizen, are what should be—but all too often are not—the model of American conservatism."

While hard to admire for his failures, Coolidge, with his New England accent, eccentricities, and simple virtues, is equally hard to dislike. During his presidency much of the country thought he was the right president for the time. "Coolidge was a transitional president at a transitional time," wrote the Coolidge biographer David Greenberg. "In his anxious acceptance of the era's ballyhoo and roar, in the quiet pleasure he took in beholding the fruits of American industry, in the solitary sadness he felt in trying to treasure a lost world—in all these ways he reflects and defines the 1920s."

But perhaps Coolidge's best eulogy came from one of his harshest critics, H. L. Mencken, who said after his death, "There were no thrills while he reigned, but neither were there any headaches. He had no ideas, but he was not a nuisance. . . . [H]is failings are forgotten; the country remembers only . . . that he let it alone. Well, there are worse **epitaphs** for a statesman."

An admirer of
Calvin Coolidge
wrote, he "was
distinguished for
character more
than heroic for
achievement.
His great task
was to restore
dignity and
prestige of the
Presidency when
it had reached
its lowest ebb
in our history."

TIMELINE

1872
Born July 4 in Plymouth Notch, Vermont

1895
Graduates from Amherst College

1905
Marries Grace Goodhue

1906
Elected to the Massachusetts House of Representatives

1909
Elected mayor of Northampton, Massachusetts

1911
Elected to the Massachusetts State Senate

1870

1918
Elected governor
of Massachusetts

1921
Elected vice president
of the United States

1923
Becomes the country's thirtieth president

1924
Elected president
in his own right

1933
Dies at his home
in Northampton,
Massachusetts, on
January 5

1940

GLOSSARY

abolitionist a person who advocated the end of slavery in the United States

Bonus Bill a compensation bill for World War I veterans passed by Congress over Coolidge's veto

communists people who believe in a system of government based on holding all property in common

comptroller a government official who supervises financial accounts and transactions

cum laude special citation on a college diploma meaning "with honor"

Democrat one of America's two major political parties, founded in 1828

depression a period in which an economy suffers, usually involving unemployment, falling prices, and failing businesses

electoral vote votes cast during national presidential elections by specially chosen representatives from each state who form the electoral college; electoral votes, not popular votes, decide presidential elections

epitaphs inscriptions on a tomb; brief works that praise a dead person

favorite son a person nominated as a presidential candidate at a convention by delegates from his or her home state

incumbent the current holder of an office

injury compensation money paid to a worker injured on the job

lieutenant governor the official second in rank to the governor of a state

margin the downpayment needed to obtain a loan from a stockbroker to buy stock

notary public a person granted the right to authorize such documents as contracts

★ ★ ★ ★ ★ ★ ★ ★ ★ ★ ★ ★ ★ ★ ★ ★ ★ ★ ★

pensions a fixed amount of money paid regularly to retired workers for past service

ratified officially confirmed or approved

Republican one of America's two major political parties, founded in 1854

solicitor a city officer in charge of its legal business

speculation act of investing in very risky ventures with the hope of earning a profit

stock share of a company or business that can be bought and sold

suffrage the right to vote

Teapot Dome Harding presidential scandal in which secretary of the interior Albert Fall secretly leased federal oil reserves to private corporations for money

ward a political district of a town or city

FURTHER INFORMATION

BOOKS

Doak, Robin S. *Calvin Coolidge* (Profiles of the Presidents). Mankato, MN: Compass Point Books, 2003.

Feldman, Ruth Tenzer. *Calvin Coolidge* (Presidential Leaders). Minneapolis, MN: Lerner Publishing Group, 2005.

Stein, R. Conrad. *Calvin Coolidge* (Encyclopedia of Presidents, Second Series). Danbury, CT: Children's Press, 2004.

Venezia, Mike. *Calvin Coolidge* (Getting to Know the U.S. Presidents). Danbury, CT: Children's Press, 2007.

VIDEOS AND DVDS

The American President. PBS Home Video, boxed DVD set.

The Clinging Vine/The Age of Ballyhoo (1926). Image Entertainment, DVD, 2006.

WEB SITES

American President: An Online Reference Resource
http://www.millercenter.virginia.edu/academic/americanpresident/coolidge
This informative site includes short, concise biographies of not only Coolidge, but also his wife, vice president, and all the members of his cabinet.

Calvin Coolidge: 30th President of the United States

http://www.calvin-coolidge.org

This Web site is operated by the Calvin Coolidge Memorial Foundation to dispense materials and programs to preserve Coolidge's legacy.

Presidents of the United States

http://www.presidentsusa.net/coolidge.html

This Calvin Coolidge home page links to countless Coolidge biographies, speeches, pictures, and other Web sites.

The White House

http://www.whitehouse.gov/history/presidents/cc30.html

The White House Web site features Coolidge's story as part of the ongoing tale of American presidents, from George Washington to George W. Bush.

BIBLIOGRAPHY

Anthony, Carl Sferrazza. *America's First Families*. New York: Touchstone, 2000.

Beschloss, Michael, editor. *American Heritage Illustrated History of the Presidents*. New York: Crown Publishers, 2000.

Coolidge, Calvin. *The Autobiography of Calvin Coolidge*. New York: Cosmopolitan Book Corporation, 1929.

Diller, David C. and Stephen L. Robertson. *The Presidents, First Ladies, and Vice Presidents*. Washington, DC: The Congressional Quarterly Press, 1997.

Freidel, Frank. *The Presidents of the United States of America*. Washington, DC: White House Historical Association, 1978.

Gould, Lewis L. *The Modern American Presidency*. Lawrence: University Press of Kansas, 2003.

Greenberg, David. *Calvin Coolidge*. New York: Henry Holt & Company, 2006.

Lathem, Edward Connery, ed. *Meet Calvin Coolidge: The Man Behind the Myth*. Brattleboro, VT: Stephen Greene Press, 1960.

Lindop, Edmund. *Presidents By Accident*. New York: Franklin Watts, 1991.

Whitney, David C. *The American Presidents*. Pleasantville, NY: Reader's Digest Association, 1996.

INDEX

Pages in **boldface** are illustrations.

★ ★ ★ ★ ★ ★ ★ ★ ★ ★ ★ ★ ★ ★ ★ ★ ★ ★

ABOUT THE AUTHOR

Steven Otfinoski is the author of more than 130 children's titles. He has written more than twenty-five nonfiction titles for Marshall Cavendish. Otfinoski lives in Connecticut with his wife, Beverly, an editor and high school English teacher.